GROW
YOUR OWN
NOSH

❧❧ THE MARKFIELD PROJECT ❧❧

Profits from this book will be donated to The Markfield Project which is a unique centre for children and young people with special needs and their families.

It provides somewhere for all children – especially those with physical or mental handicaps – to learn and grow together.

The Markfield Project offers:

• recreational, educational and social opportunities for children and their families in North-East London

• support for families who have to care for children with special needs.

It came into being in 1980 when the London Borough of Haringey's Community Play Service allowed a voluntary committee to have use of a former pumping station in Markfield Park.

Play activities in the building quickly identified that there was insufficient room for everything the children wanted and needed to do.

A major Urban Aid grant from the Government's Department of the Environment, generous help from the local authority and from charities helped to make a major conversion programme possible. In March 1986, the Princess of Wales declared the new Markfield Project well and truly open.

Inside the Victorian pumping station is a large play hall, a soft play room, computer facilities, changing rooms, workshops, lifts and ramps, a coffee bar, small group and meeting rooms, a kitchen and dining area and storage spaces. Outside a 6.5 acre site will be landscaped into an exciting and stimulating play environment.

With a small full-time staff and lots of willing volunteers, children are offered a wide range of play activities inside the building – not forgetting visits to places of interest in and around London.

All this costs money – which is why you might like to become a friend of the Markfield. Write to me asking details –Richard Briers, c/o The Markfield Project, Markfield Road, London N15 4RB (enclosing an SAE).

Richard Briers
and
Peter Heseltine

GROW
YOUR OWN
NOSH

DRAGON

Dragon
An imprint of the Children's Division
of the Collins Publishing Group
8 Grafton Street, London W1X 3LA

Published by Dragon Books 1987

Briers, Richard
Grow your own nosh.
1. Gardening–Juvenile literature
I. Title   II. Heseltine, Peter
635   SB457

ISBN 0–583–31011–7

Printed and bound in Great Britain by Collins, Glasgow

Set in Palatino

CONTENTS

Dear Reader,

'The Good Life' was a television programme about people doing things for themselves. That is what this book (and the Markfield) is about.

Grow Your Own Nosh explains how you can grow food and how to cook it. In this way you will see the cycle of life. You will be able to grow many of the plants and make many of the recipes by yourself, but you may need a little help from others in your family for some of them.

That is one of the themes behind the Markfield – the family. The Markfield Project is a family of people who have come together to provide opportunities for children and young people with special physical and mental needs to help them to grow and develop through their play.

Not on their own – but as part of a family.

As profits from this book will go to help the Markfield, buying a copy for your friends will help many other children to enjoy the good life.

Have fun growing – and eating

Richard Briers

Why bother to grow your own food? Because no matter how good the picture on the outside of the frozen food packet looks, there is still something rather special about vegetables which are freshly picked. It is also satisfying to see seeds sprout, flower and produce vegetables and fruits; the exercise of growing things is good for you (works up an appetite to eat it later); and the flavour and colour of your food is greatly improved.

This book tries to look at the food chain from seed to harvesting and from preparation to eating.

We have selected forty-seven vegetables, fruits, salad crops and herbs which can be grown in one season. Some will be familiar, others less so. The same is true of the recipes.

In the gardening section we have given basic advice which should be enough to get you going. The instructions are repeated each time so you do not have to look things up continually. If you need more information (or want to produce food for the local gardening show) ask for adult help. Help from an adult is also necessary when you need to control slugs or greenfly, as many of the chemicals which are poisonous to insects are harmful to people as well.

Not all the plants we will be describing have to be grown in the ground – many can be grown in grow bags, tubs, pots and even window boxes and hanging baskets!

We think that the recipes in many children's books are too simple. With help from an adult there is no reason why quite complicated and sophisticated dishes cannot be produced, particularly for special occasions. Often the dish is one of the ingredients in a main meal because we think it is fun for everyone to be involved in the kitchen – in most homes, children and adults spend more time in the kitchen than in any other room.

Our food today comes from many different countries. Take a look at the shelves in your supermarket or local shop and you will see the tins, packets and fresh produce come from almost every country in the world. Even plants we think of as being native to this country have often been brought here – the Romans introduced many familiar herbs which once grew only around the Mediterranean. The origins of some of the plants can be found in the odd facts we include as one of the items in each recipe.

Before you start growing – or cooking – read the next few pages. They will explain some of the terms used and include additional handy tips.

Growing things

Where

If you are lucky and have a garden, see if you can be given a small corner to grow things in. Make sure it is not in the shade behind the potting shed, but in the sun! If you have to tuck it away, can it be behind a screen of runner beans or Jerusalem artichokes?

Providing you dig the soil well, add the right amount of manure and fertilisers to get what professional gardener's call 'a good tilth' – we call it good rich soil – you can grow a lot of things in a 3 metre square plot.

If you plan your garden properly many different types of plants can be grown in small quantities. If you want to grow a sackful of potatoes – leave it to someone else! They take a lot of space and are quite hard work.

If you do not have a garden, you may still be able to grow things in the ground by persuading your teacher to let the class have a corner of the school playing field. (You can always grow tomatoes to throw at the losing team!)

If you cannot find a piece of land, you can grow quite a lot of plants in a grow-bag, tub, barrel or even a hanging basket. If the worst comes to the worst, then grow herbs in a pot on the windowsill or bean sprouts in the airing cupboard!

Tools

Anyone whose family already has a garden will have some basic gardening tools. These are the ones you need:

1 small spade

1 hoe

1 trowel

1 dibber (not a relation of Officer Dibble in 'Top Cat', but a thick, pointed stick. Make one from a broken spade or fork handle)

1 rake

1 bucket

2 sticks and a length of string (to make sure your rows are straight. Ploughmen win prizes for getting their furrows in neat lines)

Plenty of plant pots (or yoghurt cartons), peat pots, seed trays (or ice-cream containers), a sheet or two of glass, cotton, and string.

What

There is only room for us to include forty-seven plants although there are many others. Some – like apples and pears – take more than one season to grow or the seeds are a little difficult to find, other than at a good garden centre. Next time you pass one, have a look at some of the seed packets – there may be something you could grow which we have not thought of.

Seed packets will tell you also about the many different varieties of each vegetable, some of which require special conditions to grow properly. This can be quite useful; some tomatoes grow as small bushes – some are even yellow. Because you will not have a lot of space, sow varieties for flavour rather than heavy cropping.

If you are not sure what kind of plants to get, ask the people at the garden centre. They are there to help you, and they know a lot about growing things. You could ask them if they have a special children's section, and not just a collection of pretty flower seeds.

If there is no garden centre or shop in your area, talk to your neighbours, especially those who enjoy gardening. Most adults will be only too happy to help, and may lend you a few seeds or runner beans.

When

It is quite easy to tell you when to plant things inside and when to start seeds off, but more difficult outside. The weather varies from year to year and plants like runner beans require warm soil, so a cold spring can mean later planting outside. We have given dates in the book for each vegetable, but if you live in the north of England or Scotland, plant a fortnight later than the dates we suggest. Ask keen gardeners who live nearby when it is safe to plant outside.

How

Growing things is not awfully difficult, especially if you are lucky enough to have green fingers! Many gardening books and television programmes make it appear so complicated that only a Professor of Nuclear Physics is qualifed to plant a bean. If we can, anyone can!

Plants are like children – they need plenty of food, water, room to move about and lots of love and attention!

Although there are one or two exceptions, most plants need:

SOIL

To improve the soil you need to dig it well, preferably in the Autumn, breaking up the lumps so the frost can reduce them to a fine soil (or start with peas and beans – they need a firm soil so you don't have to dig). If you can mix in some farmyard manure it will make the plants hop about a bit, even if it *is* a bit pongy. (If it is horse manure, try and let it rot over winter otherwise you can end up with a garden full of buttercups or whatever it was the horse ate last!)

Failing that, use garden compost or, if really desperate, a bucketful of peat and a handful of granular fertiliser will suffice. Some plants need extra food to make them grow well – usually disgusting things like hoof and horn, dried blood and fish manure!

As they grow, many plants like a little boost – which means adding some liquid fertiliser or a 'mulch' (if you tell your teacher you were late for school because you had to mulch your beans, he or she will be very impressed).

WATER

Plants must have water to live, but you *can* drown them, and the correct amount is sometimes difficult to judge. When the leaves wilt, it is really too late (but water anyway, the plant may recover). As a general rule a good soaking with a hose pipe for half an hour once a week is better than a quick sprinkle with the watering can for plants in the garden (you will need to check that you can use a hosepipe and, if it is required, have a licence).

With plants such as marrows and tomatoes, sink a plant pot beside them and fill it with water – this will take moisture directly to the roots.

Plants in grow-bags, tubs, pots and other containers must have more frequent watering – daily in hot weather. Make sure there are holes in the bottom of the container or plastic bag to let out excess water. Some, like tomatoes, appreciate a spray as well.

SPACE

Plants like quite a lot of room to grow, so sowing the correct distance apart is important. Weeds are hoed up or removed because they compete for space, food and water.

MEDICAL CARE

Garden and container plants seem to attract all manner of horrible diseases and pests, so first aid may be required!

For diseases – technical things like wilt, black spot (sounds like something from Treasure Island), and mould – get adult advice.

For the creepy-crawlies, there are a number of remedies. Some insects are beneficial and should be encouraged – ladybirds eat greenfly, bees pollinate flowers, butterflies are beautiful. Those you can do without are the ones that eat plants – cabbage white butterfly caterpillars can make a leaf look like lace in an hour or so.

Slugs and snails can be removed by hand (but don't throw them over the fence, the neighbours only throw them back and it puzzles the snails). Some insects can be deterred by planting – tansy in amongst the beans discourages several insects. Flies and spiders can be washed off with soapy water and there are a number of natural pesticides on the market which can be used.

Safety

The garden can be a dangerous place so here are some health and safety tips:

- wear stout boots or shoes when you are digging – especially if using a fork
- tidy things away – otherwise you may trip over them and fall face first into the manure
- if you must use pesticides, follow the instructions and wash carefully afterwards.

Technical terms

Drills are shallow trenches which are made by raking the earth very finely and then pulling the corner edge of the hoe along the surface in a straight line.

Harden off means taking seedlings from indoors to the garden gradually over one or two weeks. Keep them in the shade and bring them in at night.

Pea sticks are the twiggy ends of branches which are stuck into the ground to provide support for peas and beans.

Mulch means a 2–3 cm layer of grass cuttings, straw or

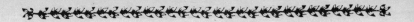

compost round the plant to conserve moisture and give nutrients. (Black polythene laid in strips will also conserve moisture in very dry weather.)

Cooking things

We think there is something rather special about cooking. The results can be super to eat, but it is also a companionable activity which you can do with your friends or family. It can be artistic as well – especially when you have to decorate something.

Starting

- make sure you have plenty of elbow room – there is nothing worse than trying to prepare food in a great clutter or a very small space.
- make sure everything is clean before you start – that includes surfaces, dishes, tools and utensils – and your hands.
- make sure you have all the ingredients before you start cooking.
- weigh things carefully – it is only professional chefs who throw in a handful of this and a handful of that!
- wear an apron to protect your clothes and use an oven cloth to protect your hands.

Preparing food

- vegetables should be washed thoroughly to remove all the soil and any creepy-crawlies, especially if you are a vegetarian.
- use a proper peeler if you are peeling vegetables and wash them afterwards as well.
- try to stick to natural ingredients and reduce the amount of salt and sugar you use.

Cooking

OVEN TEMPERATURES
Temperatures are given in °Centigrade. Here are the equivalents in Gas Marks and Fahrenheit.

Gas Mark	Fahrenheit	Centigrade
1/4	240	116
1/2	275	136
1	290	143
2	310	154
3	340	171
4	360	182
5	380	193
6	400	204
7	435	224
8	460	238
9	480	250

SAFETY

• boiling water or fat can be very dangerous – make sure an adult is present and tells you how it should be done.

• if the fat catches fire, turn the heat off and cover the pan with a wet tea towel.

• saucepan handles should point inwards so that you don't knock hot pans off the cooker.

• many vegetables are best if they are steamed rather than boiled – this helps to keep them crisp and retains the vitamins and flavour. We have a useful metal thing (called a trivet) which opens up like a flower and fits any saucepan – or you can use a metal colander or special steamer.

• sauces and gravies can go a bit lumpy if you are not careful. A lot of stirring (or a quick spin in the food processor) will get rid of these. The best way of making a smooth sauce is to add a little liquid at a time and stir it in thoroughly rather than beating it to death afterwards.

Finishing

• when you finish using tools and utensils, put them into hot water – this will make them easier to wash up.

• when hot dishes are ready, serve them immediately on plates which have been warmed.

ALPINE STRAWBERRIES

Ideal conditions	Semi-shade or pot
Time taken	6 months
Sow in	March

These mini-strawberries can be grown in pots or even in the flower border and give fruit throughout the summer and autumn. There are two main varieties which we have grown – red ones and white ones (which are said to taste of pineapple).

Alpine strawberries need well-manured soil – one bucketful of compost or a handful of granular fertiliser per square metre dug in about three weeks before planting. Just before planting out add two handfuls of fish manure and rake in.

In March, sow the seed in seed compost in a greenhouse or on a warm windowsill. Cover the seed with a light sprinkling of soil and water sparingly (about once a week, but the soil must not be allowed to dry out) until they germinate – about two or three weeks.

When the seedlings are about 2cm high, re-plant into single pots or seed trays (about 3–4cm apart). By the middle of April, the small plants should be **hardened off** (see p. 14).

In mid-May they should be ready for planting out in rows (about 20cm apart) or potted up (one per 15cm pot). Feed with a liquid fertiliser and water well if in pots.

Strawberries and Ice-cream

(Per person)
This is an extremely simple – yet delicious – way of enjoying these mini-strawberries.

> 1 handful of strawberries
> 1 scoop or portion of vanilla ice-cream
> Icing sugar

- Rinse and shake the strawberries dry in a colander or sieve.
- Sprinkle on top of ice-cream.
- Dust with icing sugar by shaking a **little** sugar through a sieve.

Did you know?

Alpine strawberries are very popular on the Continent and in Scandinavia where they grow wild in woods, in fields and on rocky outcrops.

ASPARAGUS PEAS

Ideal conditions	Sheltered sunny position, any soil or container
Time taken	3–4 months
Sow in	April–May

These curious peas have a faint flavour of asparagus – hence their name. You eat them whole – pods and all!

Asparagus peas need well-manured soil – one bucketful of compost or a handful of granular fertiliser per square metre dug in about three weeks before planting. Just before sowing add two handfuls of fish manure and rake in.

Make a drill about 2cm deep and plant the peas 20cm apart. Cover them lightly with soil. As birds are partial to pea seedlings, protect them by stretching cotton tied to sticks over the top of the pea patch.

As they grow, the peas will need support, and you can provide this by pushing pea sticks into the ground by the side of the plants or by fixing a 5cm netting over the row and winding the plants through it.

Water them well in dry weather and mulch them.

Pick the pods when they are 4cm long – by harvesting regularly, a continual crop of pea pods will be ensured.

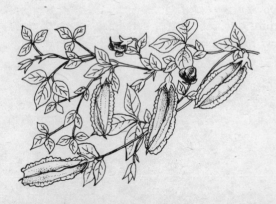

Buttered Pea Pods

(4 people)

Many vegetables taste and look better if the cooking is simple and not over fussy – especially if there are strongly flavoured sauces or gravy with the main course.

> 1 lb asparagus pea pods
> 1 cup of water
> 1 oz butter/margarine
> Freshly ground pepper

- Wash the pea pods thoroughly.
- Place them in a saucepan with sufficient boiling water to cover the bottom of the pan and cook until they are tender, but still firm. Steam if possible.
- Drain in a colander, place them back in the pan and shake over a gentle heat until they are dry.
- Place them in a serving dish, dot the top with butter/margarine, add some freshly ground pepper and serve.

Did you know?

Within half an hour of harvesting, vegetables lose 25% of their vitamins – slicing them loses even more and boiling them loses almost half their Vitamin C.

Ideal conditions	Grow-bags or rich soil in a warm sheltered position
Time taken	6 months
Sow in	March

Aubergines are often known as eggplants and are usually grown in hot countries. In colder countries they will grow in a greenhouse, outside in a hot summer or even in a 25cm pot on a sunny windowsill.

If they are not to be grown in a container or grow-bag, aubergines need well-manured soil – one bucketful of compost or a handful of granular fertiliser per square metre dug in about three weeks before planting. Just before sowing add two handfuls of fish manure and rake in.

Sow the seeds in John Innes potting compost in a seed tray or yoghurt pots in March, barely cover the seed, and water lightly. Cover with a sheet of glass and a newspaper.

When the seeds have germinated, remove the newspaper and the glass to let the plants grow. Keep the compost moist until the plants are ready to plant out in June. Plant three to a grow-bag or 45cm apart in the ground.

Spray the flowers with water from a plant spray each evening to help them make fruit.

When they are 30cm high, pinch out the tips of each plant so they bush out. Support each branch as it grows by tying it to a frame. Let one flower only form on each branch (there are usually about five per plant) so that good-sized aubergines will grow.

When the aubergines have reached the size of ping-pong balls, feed the plant with a liquid fertiliser (follow the manufacturer's instructions). Keep the soil moist and cut the aubergines when they are about 20cm long.

Recipe

Aubergine Fritters

(4 people)

There are several vegetables which can be cooked in this way, including cauliflowers, leeks, onions, mushrooms and crisp-thin potato slices. As the recipe requires a pan of hot oil, ask for adult help.

1 lb aubergines
4 oz wholemeal flour
½ teaspoon of salt
¼ pint of milk
1 egg
Oil

- Wash and peel the aubergine and slice it into pieces 1cm thick.
- Place them in a saucepan with sufficient boiling water to cover them and cook for five minutes. Better still, steam them.
- Drain in a colander, place them back in the pan and shake over a gentle heat until they are dry.
- Make a batter mix by whisking together the flour, salt, milk and egg.
- Heat the oil in a frying or chip pan. (It is ready when a drop of batter mix whizzes round the pan like a firework.)
- Dip the aubergine slices in batter to coat them and fry them until they are golden brown.
- Lift them out and drain them on a piece of kitchen paper.

Did you know?

If left before cooking, the aubergine slices will go brown. Keep them in water containing a teaspoonful of lemon juice – or even white wine.

Ideal conditions	Indoors in a pot or in a sunny, sheltered position
Time taken	2 months
Sow in	May

Basil is a herb which originally came from India, so it requires plenty of sun and protection from frosts. There are two main varieties – sweet basil and bush basil. Sweet basil is the best one for cooking.

Fill a seed tray with potting compost and firm it down. Mix the seed with an equal amount of sand, sprinkle it thinly over the surface and cover lightly with soil. Water sparingly.

Place a sheet of glass over the top, cover that with newspaper and place on a windowsill. Remove the glass each day and wipe off the drops of condensation. When the seeds germinate take off the paper and glass.

As soon as the seeds are large enough to handle, re-pot them into 15cm pots or, in June, to a sunny, sheltered spot in the garden. The pots can be kept indoors or outdoors.

When the flower buds appear, pinch them off to encourage the plant to produce more leaves.

Recipe

Baked Tomatoes

(4 people)

Basil is a lovely warm-smelling herb which should be used fresh. It goes especially well with tomatoes, so try making this tasty lunch-time snack.

> ½ lb mushrooms
> 1 lb tomatoes
> 2 tablespoons chopped basil leaves
> Freshly ground pepper
> 3 oz wholemeal breadcrumbs
> 2 oz butter/margarine

- Preheat the oven to 200°C.
- Clean the mushrooms and slice them thinly.
- Wash and slice the tomatoes into ½cm slices.
- Grease an ovenproof dish with a little butter or margarine.
- Place alternate layers of mushrooms and tomatoes in the dish, ending with a layer of tomatoes. Sprinkle the chopped basil and pepper on each layer of tomato.
- Spread the breadcrumbs over the top and dot with pats of butter or margarine.
- Bake in the oven for 25 minutes and serve with wholemeal bread.

Did you know?

Sweet basil is disliked by flies and a basil plant kept in a pot on the windowsill will keep them away.

BEAN SPROUTS

Ideal conditions	Warm, dark place
Time taken	5–7 days
Sow in	Any time

These are grown from special beans which can be found in health food shops or in some garden centres. The most common ones are grown from mung beans.

Find a large empty jam jar and wash and clean it thoroughly. Fill one sixth of it with beans, cover them with luke warm water and leave overnight.

The next day, pour out the water. Cover the top with muslin or cheesecloth held on by an elastic band. Turn the jar upside down to get rid of any excess moisture and place it in a warm place (try the airing cupboard).

Each morning and evening, pour luke warm water into the jar and turn it upside down so the water drains away.

The beans and shoots are ready to eat when the shoots are about 1–1.5cm long. By this time the beans should have filled the whole jar!

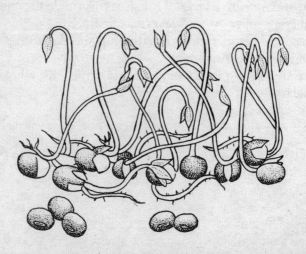

Recipe

Bean Sprout Salad

(4 people)

One of the nicest things about salads is that they can be made to look good enough to eat by combining different coloured vegetables. Here is one that is suitable to enter for an Art Exhibition!

> 4 oz bean sprouts
> 4 sticks of celery
> 4 oz mushrooms
> 2 oz green peppers
> 2 oz red peppers
> 2 oz yellow peppers
> 4 oz carrots
> 10 black grapes
> Marigold petals
> Borage flowers

- Wash all the ingredients.
- Cut open the peppers and remove the seeds.
- Chop the celery and peppers into very small cubes.
- Peel and grate the carrot.
- Slice the mushrooms thinly.
- Quarter and de-pip the grapes.
- Mix it all together.
- Store in a cool place or refrigerator for an hour.
- Decorate with marigold petals and borage flowers and serve.

Did you know?

In a few days the vitamins in the bean sprouts will have increased by almost 750%. There are 13 major vitamins which are needed to help the body work properly and grow well.

Ideal conditions	Light soil
Time taken	10 weeks
Sow in	April

This member of the beet family is best known for its bright red colour and is often eaten cold with salads.

Beetroot need well-manured soil – one bucketful of compost or a handful of granular fertiliser per square metre dug in about three weeks before planting. Just before sowing add two handfuls of fish manure and rake in.

Make a drill 2.5cm deep and place the seeds 10cm apart along the row. Cover the seeds with soil, rake gently and firm the earth down with the back of the rake.

As each seed is really a cluster of seeds, many seedlings will pop up. After a month thin out the smallest ones to leave just one plant.

When the root is about the size of a ping-pong ball, pull up alternate ones (you can eat them in salads) and leave the remainder to grow to the size of tennis balls.

You have to be careful when you pull them up – if the skin breaks, the beetroot will bleed and lose its colour.

Did you know?

There are several different kinds of beet grown by farmers – two common ones are sugar beet, used for making sugar and mangel-wurzels (Latin name Beta Vulgaris Vulgaris which means it is extremely common!) used for feeding cattle.

Recipe

Polish Beetroot

(4 people)
This is a nice, sharply-flavoured recipe with an unusual taste.

2 lb beetroot
1 small onion
½ oz butter/margarine
½ oz wholemeal flour
1 small carton plain yoghurt
2 teaspoons grated horseradish
Freshly ground pepper
Chopped parsley

- Wash the beetroot carefully, taking care not to break the skin.
- Place them in a saucepan with sufficient boiling water to cover them. Cook for about 30 minutes until almost tender.
- Drain the beetroot and, when it has cooled, rub or peel off the skin.
- Grate the beetroot.
- Peel and chop the onion into small pieces.
- Fry it in butter/margarine until soft and golden in colour.
- Stir in the flour, then the yoghurt and bring back to the boil.
- Add the beetroot and horseradish and simmer for 10 minutes.
- Season with freshly ground pepper.
- Place in a serving dish, sprinkle with chopped parsley and serve.

Ideal conditions	Anywhere in the garden or a grow-bag
Time taken	3 months
Sow in	March

Fresh broad beans straight from the pod are a delicious vegetable, and some of the bushy varieties can be grown in small gardens or containers.

Broad beans need well-manured soil – one bucketful of compost or a handful of granular fertiliser per square metre dug in about three weeks before planting. Just before sowing add two handfuls of fish manure and rake in.

Make holes 5cm deep and 15cm apart (or six per grow-bag), pop a broad bean into each and re-fill the hole.

Cut off any shoots which appear from the base.

When the beans are in full flower, pinch out the top to discourage blackfly. If they still come, wash the top with soapy water or use a pesticide (follow the manufacturer's instructions).

When the beans inside the pod are about the size of a 1p coin, they are ready for picking. If left too long they become tough to eat – but let some grow and dry off to plant for next year's crop. The roots should be left in the ground as they replace nitrogen for next year's sowings.

Recipe

Bacon and Bean Pasta

(4 people)
Pork or bacon and beans complement each other, so try this
quick lunch-time snack.

> 1 onion
> 1 stick of celery
> 1 tablespoon olive or other cooking oil
> 4 oz bacon
> ½ lb shelled broad beans
> 1 lb pasta shells
> 1 egg
> Freshly ground pepper
> Grated Parmesan or Cheddar cheese

- Chop the onion and celery into small pieces.
- Fry them in the oil until almost tender.
- Chop the bacon and add it to the pan.
- Add the shelled beans.
- Cook gently, stirring constantly until the beans have softened.
- Meanwhile, cook the pasta shells in boiling water until soft.
- Drain the pasta and shake it dry.
- Mix the pasta into the pan with the other ingredients and remove from the heat.
- Beat the egg in a cup, pour it over the pasta mix and stir in. Serve immediately with freshly ground pepper and grated cheese over the top.

Did you know?

Green pasta is made by adding puréed spinach to the pasta
dough. Puréed tomato makes an orangey/red pasta.

BROCCOLI

Ideal conditions	Sunny open position
Time taken	10 months
Sow in	April-May

The flowers of broccoli, which are the nicest part to eat, come in two colours – purple and green – so for the greatest artistic effect, grow both sorts. Having different coloured vegetables on your plate makes the meal look good enough to eat.

Broccoli needs well-manured soil – one bucketful of compost or a handful of granular fertiliser per square metre dug in about three weeks before planting. Just before sowing add two handfuls of fish manure and rake in.

Make a seed-bed by digging and raking the soil so it is very fine and free of stones and weeds. Make a drill 1cm deep, mix the seeds with an equal quantity of sand and sow thinly along the row. Cover, firm down with the back of a rake and water sparingly.

When the seedlings are about 8cm high, transplant them. Make a hole with a dibber 1cm deeper than the seedling and 75cm apart. Fill the hole with water and let it drain away before popping the seedling in. Re-fill the hole and tread the soil down firmly.

A month after planting, add a handful of hoof and horn fertiliser and a handful of granular fertiliser per square metre.

In the Autumn, draw earth around the plant stems by making a furrow on either side. This helps to keep them firm in the winter winds and provide additional drainage.

As the flower heads develop, cut off the top one to encourage side shoots. For eating, the heads and top leaves should be cut just before the flowers open.

Did you know?

Bacteria have to break down hoof and horn fertilisers to provide nitrogen for the plant.

Broccoli Cheese

(4 persons)

This can be prepared as a side dish to a roast dinner or as a lunchtime snack like cauliflower cheese.

1 lb broccoli	1 egg
1 oz butter/margarine	2 hard-boiled eggs
2 tablespoons wholemeal flour	2 oz grated cheese
1 pint vegetable water	1 tomato
4 tablespoons plain yoghurt	Freshly ground pepper

- Wash the broccoli
- Cook in boiling water (or steam, if possible).
- Drain in a colander, keeping the water. Place the broccoli back in the pan and shake dry over a gentle heat.

Meanwhile

- Melt the butter/margarine in a saucepan. Add sufficient flour to leave the sides dry when mixed together.
- Add the vegetable water, a little at a time, stirring continuously.
- When it becomes a thick sauce, without lumps, add the yoghurt and an egg.
- Cook until smooth, stirring all the time.
- Shell and slice the hard-boiled eggs into quarters. Place them in the bottom of an oven proof dish, put the broccoli on top and pour the sauce over it.
- Sprinkle on the grated cheese and decorate with slices of tomato.
- Add the freshly ground pepper.
- Grill for 10 minutes until the cheese bubbles and browns.

BRUSSELS SPROUTS

Ideal conditions	Firm soil with lots of space
Time taken	7 months
Sow in	February/March

Brussels sprouts are one of the best sources of Vitamin C, but they need quite a lot of elbow room to grow properly.

Sprouts need well-manured soil – one/two bucketfuls of compost or two handfuls of granular fertiliser per square metre dug in about three weeks before planting. Just before sowing add two handfuls of fish manure and rake in.

Tread the soil down firmly at weekly intervals while the seeds are growing in a seed-bed elsewhere.

Make a seed-bed by digging and raking the soil until it is very fine and free of stones and weeds. Make a drill 3cm deep, mix the seed with an equal quantity of sand and sow very thinly along the row. Cover and water.

When the plants are 10–15cm high, dig them up carefully and plant them 1m apart in the prepared ground. Firm them in by standing on either side of the sprout and pressing down. Give the new planted seedling a good soaking of water.

From about October, it will be possible to cut off the bottom sprouts, although they are best left until November after the first frosts.

When the sprouts are finished, pinch out the tops and cook them like cabbage.

Recipe

Nutty Sprouts

(4 people)

This is a French recipe, which may sound a bit odd, but adds some 'oomph' to the sprouts!

> 10 sweet chestnuts
> 1 lb Brussels sprouts
> 4 oz cooked ham
> 4 tablespoons yoghurt
> Freshly ground pepper

- Preheat the oven to 175°C.
- Peel and skin the chestnuts (removing the skin is easier if the chestnut is plunged into boiling water for a few minutes).
- Cook them in the boiling water until tender. When they are cool enough to handle, chop them into small pieces.
- Remove the outer leaves from the sprouts, make a cross cut in the stem and wash them.
- Place them in a saucepan with sufficient boiling water to cover the bottom (steam them if possible) and cook until almost tender.
- Drain the sprouts in a colander.
- Chop the ham into 1cm squares.
- Mix all the ingredients including the yoghurt into an oven proof casserole, season with pepper.
- Cover with lid or cooking foil and cook in the centre of the oven for 10 minutes.

Did you know?

The Brussels sprout really is named after the capital city of Belgium where it is said to originate.

CRITICAL
BUTTER BEANS

Ideal conditions	Sunny position or grow-bag
Time taken	4–6 months
Sow in	May

Few people grow butter or Lima beans in this country although they are very popular in Canada and America. They can be eaten with their pods when young or, if left to mature, dried for use in soups and stews.

Butter beans need well-manured soil – one bucketful of compost or a handful of granular fertiliser per square metre dug in about three weeks before planting. Just before sowing add two handfuls of fish manure and rake in.

In mid-May sow the beans in 8cm peat pots, or yoghurt cartons and place them in a warm dark place to germinate (try the airing cupboard). When they have sprouted, bring them back into the light, protecting them from frost.

From the middle of June they are ready for planting outside, 15cm apart. Bush varieties will need pea sticks to support them. Climbing varieties like runner beans require posts and bean netting.

In dry weather give the beans a good soaking once a week. They should not be fed since this encourages the plant to produce leaves instead of beans.

If you want dried butter beans, leave the pods until late October. Take the beans from the pods and dry them on a tray in the airing cupboard. Store them in a cool, well-ventilated place.

Recipe

Butter Bean Casserole

(4 people)

This is a side-dish which goes well with a bacon or pork joint, but remember that the beans need to be soaked overnight.

> 8 oz dried butter beans
> 20 shallots
> 2 oz butter/margarine
> 1 teaspoon dried or chopped fresh savory
> 1 pint chicken stock
> 2–3 blades of mace
> ¼ pint plain yoghurt
> Freshly grated pepper
> Chopped parsley

- Place the beans in a bowl, cover with boiling water and leave overnight.
- Preheat the oven to 180°C.
- Wash the shallots and take off the outer skin.
- Place the butter/margarine in a flame-proof casserole and brown the shallots over a gentle heat.
- Add the beans, savory, mace and stock.
- When the beans are tender and the stock is almost absorbed, stir in the yoghurt and cook for a further 10 minutes.
- Sprinkle with chopped parsley and freshly ground pepper and serve.

Did you know?

Butter beans are a good source of fibre. Fibre-rich foods are important for good health as they help the body rid itself of waste materials.

CABBAGE

Ideal conditions	Sunny position
Time taken	8–9 months
Sow in	March–April

Cabbages can be grown most of the year round, providing the right variety is sown. These details are for winter cabbages.

Cabbages need well-manured soil – one bucketful of compost or a handful of granular fertiliser per square metre dug in about three weeks before planting. Just before sowing add two handfuls of fish manure and rake in.

Make a drill 2cm deep and sow three seeds every 30cm along the row. Cover and water thoroughly. When the seedlings are about 5cm high, remove the weakest ones in each group.

They need little extra care other than watering thoroughly once a week in dry weather and picking off caterpillars or spraying whitefly with insecticide (follow the manufacturer's instructions).

Cut the cabbages when the hearts are firm – you can leave them in the ground until February, using them as required.

Cabbage and Raisins

(4 people)
Cabbage is a much misunderstood vegetable – most people overcook it and serve it as a soggy and unappetising mess. It should be taken from the saucepan of boiling water (or steamer) while still crisp – what the Italians call 'al dente' (in English it means 'to the tooth').

> 1 cabbage
> ¼ pint water
> 1 oz butter/margarine
> 2 oz raisins
> Freshly ground pepper

- Chop the cabbage leaves up into 1cm strips and then into 2cm pieces. Wash well and shake dry.
- Bring the water to the boil and add the butter/margarine.
- Add the cabbage and cook, stirring frequently, until almost tender.
- Wash the raisins and add them after 10 minutes.
- Remove from the heat, drain, add the freshly ground pepper and serve.

Did you know?

Raisins are dried grapes.

CARROTS

Ideal conditions	Any soil, deep box, tub or barrel
Time taken	3 months
Sow in	March onwards

This popular and colourful root vegetable is full of vitamins and minerals.

Carrots should be grown quickly, and a light, sandy soil is best. In a container, use John Innes potting compost number 1 or 2. Carrots will grow quite happily (have you ever seen a miserable carrot?) in heavier soil, but take longer to grow because the soil takes longer to warm up.

Sprinkle a handful of granular fertiliser per square metre and rake it into the top 2cm of soil.

Make a shallow drill about 50mm deep. Mix the seed with an equal quantity of sand and sprinkle the mixture thinly along the row. Cover it lightly with soil, and water it. (The same method applies for a tub or container.)

When the carrots come up, thin the seedlings to 4cm apart.

Pull them out of the ground for cooking while they are young and sweet, but not too small to handle.

Carrot and Apple Salad

(4 people)

This makes a tasty, crunchy salad to have with a snack for summer lunch.

> 4 large carrots
> 2 large eating apples
> 2 oz sultanas
> 2 oz chopped walnuts
> ½ lemon
> Freshly ground pepper
> 1 tablespoon chopped parsley

- Peel and grate the carrots.
- Peel, core and chop the apples into small pieces.
- Wash and dry the sultanas.
- Mix the apple and carrot together with the sultanas and walnuts.
- Squeeze the lemon with a lemon squeezer and add the juice to the salad.
- Season with pepper.
- Sprinkle chopped parsley over the top, chill for an hour and serve.

Did you know?

Carrot fly can be a pest with carrots – so plant sage near the carrots as flies dislike its smell.

Ideal conditions	Open, sheltered position
Time taken	6 months
Sow in	February

There are many different sorts of cauliflowers, so look for the mini-ones which are easier to grow and demand less space.

Cauliflowers need well-manured soil – one bucketful of compost or a handful of granular fertiliser per square metre dug in about three weeks before planting. Just before sowing add two handfuls of fish manure and rake in.

Place potting compost in a seed tray, firm it down and sprinkle the seeds thinly. Cover lightly with soil and water sparingly. Cover with a sheet of glass and a newspaper. When the seeds germinate, remove the glass and paper.

The seedlings are ready for potting into 6cm peat pots when they have two leaves and for sowing outside in April when they have six leaves.

Make a row of holes 45cm apart with the dibber, each one the depth of a seedling. Fill each hole with water and let it drain away. Put a seedling in the hole and re-fill it. Firm it down and keep it well-watered for the first two or three weeks, especially in dry weather.

Once a month, spread a handful of soot, dried blood or nitrate of soda per square metre. A 3cm mulch of grass clippings will help to conserve moisture.

As the white curds grow, bend the leaves over to stop the sunlight discolouring them.

Did you know?

The cauliflower head is really lots of small flowers.

Recipe

Cauliflower Cheese

(4 people)
Make this as a lunch-time dish for the family.

> 1 large cauliflower (or equivalent small heads)
> 2 oz butter/margarine
> 2 oz wholemeal flour
> 1 pint milk
> 4 oz grated Cheddar cheese
> 1 tablespoon Dijon mustard
> 2 hard-boiled eggs
> 1 tomato
> Freshly ground pepper

- Cut the leaves from the cauliflower and chop the florets into similar bite-sized pieces.
- Place them in a saucepan with sufficient boiling water to cover the bottom and cook until tender. If possible, steam them.

Meanwhile
- Melt the butter/margarine in a saucepan. Add sufficient flour to leave the sides dry when mixed together.
- Add the milk, a little at a time, stirring continuously.
- When it becomes a thick sauce, without lumps, add ¾ of the cheese and all the mustard.
- Cook until smooth, stirring all the time.

- Grease an oven proof dish with butter or margarine.
- Quarter the hard-boiled eggs, place them at the bottom of the dish, cover with cauliflower and pour on the sauce.
- Sprinkle grated cheese on top, decorate with sliced tomato and add the freshly ground pepper.
- Grill until the cheese bubbles and browns.

CELERY

Ideal conditions	Any soil
Time taken	9 months
Sow in	April

Celery is a little complicated to grow, although there are self-blanching varieties which make life a lot easier. It is an essential vegetable in the kitchen and is used in many different salads and other dishes.

The soil requires some preparation. In January, dig a trench 45cm wide and 40cm deep, piling the earth on either side. Place a 15cm layer of well-rotted compost or farmyard manure in the bottom, put 15cm of soil on top and let it settle. In March, add a handful of fish manure per metre.

At the end of March, fill a seed tray with potting compost, sprinkle the seeds on to the top and lightly cover with soil. Water, cover with a sheet of newspaper and stand the tray on a windowsill.

When the seedlings emerge, remove the newspaper and let them grow to about 10cm high.

In June, make a hole in the trench with a dibber, pop in the seedling, re-fill and firm down. Water very thoroughly. Celery roots should not dry out so they will need watering regularly in dry weather.

Feed them each week with a liquid manure (follow the manufacturer's instructions).

If you are not growing a self-blanching variety, the celery will have to be earthed up. When it is about 30cm high, hold the top together and make a sloping earth mound round it. Do this at monthly intervals.

Recipe

Waldorf Salad

(4 people)
This is a luxury salad served in small quantities. It was invented at the Waldorf Astoria Hotel in New York.

2 sticks of celery
2 eating apples
4 oz chopped walnuts
6 tablespoons mayonnaise
Freshly ground pepper
Paprika

- Wash the celery and chop it into small pieces.
- Peel, core and chop the apples into small pieces.
- Mix together in a bowl with the chopped walnuts and the mayonnaise.
- Season with freshly ground pepper.
- Decorate with a pinch of paprika sprinkled over the top.
- Chill in a refrigerator for an hour before serving.

Did you know?

Paprika is made from ground sweet red peppers and is extremely popular in Hungary – it is often called Hungarian paprika.

CHICORY

Ideal conditions	Well-drained soil
Time taken	7–8 months
Sow in	May

You have to grow this curious salad vegetable twice – it is the shoots which you eat when they sprout for the second time.

Chicory needs well-manured soil – one bucketful of compost or a handful of granular fertiliser per square metre dug in about three weeks before planting. Just before sowing add two handfuls of fish manure and rake in.

If the ground does not already contain chalk or lime (ask an adult), add a handful of carbonate of lime every square metre.

Make a drill 1cm deep, mix the seed with a similar amount of sand and scatter it thinly along the row. Water sparingly.

When the seedlings have grown three leaves, thin them out to 20cm apart. Water two or three times a week in dry weather.

As the leaves die back in late October/early November, dig the roots up and keep those which are about 5cm at the top and over 20cm long. Cut away the remaining leaves and trim the root back to 20cm long.

Place a root in a 10cm plant pot and cover it with sand, moist potting compost or peat. Water sparingly. Put a black polythene bag over the top and store it in a warm, dark place – the airing cupboard will do. Keep moist.

When the shoots are about 15cm long (about 6 weeks) they are ready for eating.

Recipe

Chicory and Stilton

This is a stunning creation for a party – make sure you sample some because it will disappear very quickly, it is so delicious.

> 2 hard-boiled egg yolks
> 2 oz Blue Stilton cheese
> 2 oz butter/margarine
> Freshly ground pepper
> 1 head of chicory
> Handful of parsley sprigs
> ¼ teaspoon paprika

- Push the egg yolks into a bowl through a sieve using the back of a wooden spoon.
- Add the cheese and butter/margarine and mash together with a fork.
- Season with pepper.
- Separate the chicory into individual leaves.
- Fill each leaf with the egg mixture and fold it up.
- Place the leaves on a dish and decorate with parsley sprigs and sprinkled paprika.

Did you know?

Stilton was first sold at the Bell Inn in the village of Stilton which is on the Great North Road (the A1) in Huntingdonshire.

CHIVES

Ideal conditions	Semi-shade or plant pot
Time taken	2–3 months
Sow in	March

The chive is a member of the onion family, but it is the leaves rather than the bulbs which are used. Although treated as a herb it is not a true one. It can be grown quite effectively as an edging plant in a flower border or along a path.

In the garden, make a drill 1cm deep. Mix the seed with an equal amount of sand, sprinkle thinly along the row and cover. Plant in a similar way in an 18cm plant pot. Keep well watered and weed by hand.

Once a month feed with a liquid fertiliser (follow the manufacturer's instructions).

When the chive starts to produce flowers, cut them off to encourage a continual supply of leaves. For use in the kitchen, cut leaves to about 5cm above ground level.

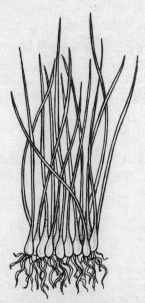

Recipe

Chive Potatoes

(4 people)
Chives have many uses in the kitchen – mixed with cottage cheese they make good sandwich fillers, and they can be added to stews, casseroles and salads.

> 4 large potatoes
> 1 oz butter/margarine
> 1 tablespoon plain yoghurt
> 2 oz grated cheese
> Large handful chopped chives

- Preheat the oven to 190°C.
- Scrub and dry the potatoes.
- Cut carefully through the skin at the top so that it looks like a lid.
- Bake for 90 minutes in the oven or until tender.
- Lift off the lid and scoop out the potato, being careful not to break the skin.
- Mash it in a bowl and mix in the remaining ingredients.
- Re-stuff the potato skins and bake for a further 15 minutes.

Did you know?

If you plant chives in the rose bed it is supposed to help the roses grow better as greenfly dislike chives.

COURGETTES

Ideal conditions	Very rich soil or grow-bag in sunny position
Time taken	5 months
Sow in	May

Courgettes are like mini-marrows and can be grown in two main colours – green and yellow. Why not try both?

Courgettes needs very well-manured soil – two bucketfuls of compost or two handfuls of granular fertiliser per square metre dug in about three weeks before planting. Just before sowing add two handfuls of fish manure and rake in.

Fill a 6cm peat pot with potting compost and push two seeds into the soil about 1cm deep at opposite sides of the pot. Make sure the pointed end of the seed is uppermost.

Put in a warm place and water sparingly.

When they germinate, remove the weakest looking seedling. At the end of May begin to harden them off and in June, when the danger of frost has passed, they will be ready for planting out in a grow-bag or in the garden.

Water them well (daily in very dry weather) and feed weekly with a liquid fertiliser (follow the manufacturer's instructions).

Pick the courgettes when they are about 15cm long.

Recipe

Courgette Salad

(4 people)

Although courgettes are mainly thought of as a hot dish, they can be equally delicious cold.

> ½ lb courgettes
> ½ lb tomatoes
> 2 tablespoons olive oil
> 1 teaspoon white wine vinegar
> 1 teaspoon lemon juice
> 1 clove garlic (crushed)
> Freshly ground pepper
> 1 tablespoon chopped chives

- Wash the courgettes and trim off the ends.
- Place the courgettes in a saucepan containing sufficient boiling water to cover them and cook for 5 minutes (steam them if you can).
- Place in a colander, rinse with cold water and drain thoroughly.
- Slice the courgettes into 1cm slices.
- Slice the tomatoes into ½cm slices.
- Mix together.
- Prepare the dressing by mixing together the oil, vinegar, lemon juice, crushed garlic and pepper.
- Pour the dressing over the courgettes and tomatoes, sprinkle with chopped chives and stir together.
- Place in a cool place or refrigerator for an hour before serving.

Did you know?

Olive oil is a healthy oil for cooking as it is low in saturated fats which are not good for you. It is used in salad dressings because of its flavour.

CUCUMBERS

Ideal conditions	Sunny position or grow-bag
Time taken	3 months
Sow in	April

Cucumbers can be grown in a greenhouse or outdoors, but you need to make sure you get the right variety – especially with the outdoor ones as some can be slightly bitter.

Whichever variety of cucumber you use, they are started in pots indoors and planted outside when all danger of frosts has passed.

If the cucumbers are to be planted outside, prepare the soil by digging holes 1m apart and 30cm square and deep. Fill the holes with well-rotted compost or old farmyard manure and tread down to half-full. Fill the hole with earth and make a small mound.

In April, place two seeds in a 5cm plant pot filled with potting compost and place in a warm, light place such as a greenhouse or windowsill.

In mid-May, plant outside in the garden or in a grow-bag.

Pinch out the top when six leaves have formed so that side shoots will grow. As cucumbers have surface roots you should not hoe (hooray) but pull the weeds up by hand (groan). A 2–3cm mulch will help to conserve moisture.

The cucumbers will need watering once a week in dry weather (daily in a grow-bag, but do not let them get waterlogged). When the first cucumbers are about 8cm long, feed them with a liquid fertiliser (follow the manufacturer's instructions).

Mint and Cucumber Salad

(4 people)

This is a dish which is sharp and cool – an ideal starter for a meal on a summer day when you have finished all that gardening.

> 1 cucumber
> 2 small cartons of plain yoghurt
> 1 teaspoon chopped mint leaves
> 1 teaspoon chopped parsley
> 1 tomato, quartered
> Freshly ground pepper

- Peel the cucumber and dice it very small.
- Mix it with the chopped mint leaves and yoghurt.
- Sprinkle chopped parsley on top and decorate with tomato quarters. Sprinkle with freshly ground pepper.
- Place in a cool place for an hour before serving.

Did you know?

The posh name for a starter (the dish served before the main course) is an 'hors-d'oeuvre'. They are usually light, decorative dishes which enable you to show off your artistic ability as well as your culinary skill.

FENNEL

Ideal conditions	Sheltered sunny spot with well-drained soil
Time taken	5–6 months
Sow in	April–May

Fennel has a very strong aniseed taste – good for those who like aniseed balls, but not everyone appreciates it. The swollen bulbous parts at the bottom of the stems can be cooked or eaten raw with salads. The feathery leaves can be used in sauces (especially with fish) or for decoration.

Fennel needs well-manured soil – one bucketful of compost or a handful of granular fertiliser per square metre dug in about three weeks before planting.

Make a drill 1cm deep. Mix the seeds with an equal amount of sand and sprinkle thinly along the row. Cover the seeds lightly and water thoroughly.

Thin the seedlings out to 20cm apart when they are 4cm high.

Water thoroughly once a week in dry weather.

The stems are best if they are white, so draw earth up round them (or tie a collar of cardboard round the stem).

In the autumn dig up the fennel, cut off the stem and roots, leaving the bulbous base – that is the bit you eat!

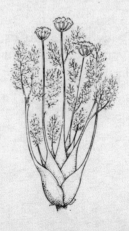

Recipe

Braised Fennel

(4 people)
Check that everyone likes the taste of aniseed or just make a small quantity to begin with.

> 1 fennel stem
> 1 carrot
> 1 onion
> 1 stick of celery
> 1 oz butter/margarine
> ½ pint chicken stock
> Freshly ground pepper

- Preheat the oven to 225°C.
- Wash the fennel and cut it into four sections.
- Place them in a saucepan of boiling water and cook for five minutes (this is called parboiling). Steam them if you can.
- Drain in a colander, return to the saucepan and shake over a gentle heat until dry.
- Scrape the carrot and chop into small pieces.
- Peel the onion and chop into small pieces.
- Scrub the celery and chop into small pieces.
- Place all the ingredients into an oven-proof dish and pour the stock over the top.
- Cover with a lid or foil and cook for 25 minutes in the oven.

Did you know?

Fennel helps to keep insects away, so a piece in the kitchen will make sure there are no flies on you! (It is reputed also to keep witches away so hang some outside your bedroom door on Halloween.)

FRENCH BEANS

Ideal conditions   Sunny position, grow-bag or pot
Time taken   3 months
Sow in   Late April–early May

These are one of the most delicious vegetables and are quite easy to grow. You can plant them in any spare space as they come up as neat little bushes.

French beans need well-manured soil – one bucketful of compost or a handful of granular fertiliser per square metre dug in about three weeks before planting. Just before sowing add two handfuls of fish manure and rake in.

French beans are also partial to a warm, dry soil so you will need to wait until the soil warms up and dries out a bit. You can plant them earlier in a grow-bag or 20cm pot filled with potting compost.

Make holes 5cm deep and 15cm apart, pop a bean into each, re-fill and firm down lightly.

If growing in a grow-bag or pot, keep the soil moist, but not saturated. Feed with a liquid manure (follow the manufacturer's instructions.)

In the garden they will need a good soak once or twice a week in dry weather. A mulch will help to conserve moisture.

The beans are ready for picking when they are about 12–15cm long. If you leave them to get larger, they will get stringy and chewy.

Boiled Beans

(4 people)

French beans are so full of flavour that only the simplest recipe is needed to produce a delicious dish. With freshly grown vegetables, the simpler the recipe the better.

> 1 lb beans
> 1 oz butter/margarine
> 1 teaspoon lemon juice
> 1 tablespoon chopped parsley
> Freshly ground pepper

- Wash the beans and trim off the ends.
- Place them in a saucepan with sufficient boiling water to cover the bottom of the pan. (Steam them if possible.)
- Cook for 15 minutes until almost tender.
- Drain in a colander, return to the saucepan and shake over a gentle heat until dry.
- Add the butter, chopped parsley, lemon juice and pepper and cook gently in the saucepan for a further 3–4 minutes.

Did you know?

If you really must have giant beans, you can now buy stringless varieties.

GARLIC

Ideal conditions	Full sun or pot
Time taken	6 months
Sow in	April

If you have been abroad on holiday – especially to France – you will know the flavour of this herb. It is extremely useful in the kitchen and is an essential ingredient in many dishes.

As a member of the onion family, it is cultivated in a very similar way. Garlic can be grown in a 15cm plant pot filled with potting compost.

If grown in the garden, garlic needs well-manured soil – one bucketful of compost or a handful of granular fertiliser per square metre dug in about three weeks before planting. Just before sowing add two handfuls of fish manure and rake in.

Split a garlic bulb into its separate pieces (these are called cloves). Make small holes in the soil about 5cm deep and 20cm apart with the end of a stick or cane. Pop the clove in, pointed end uppermost and re-fill the hole.

A grow-bag should be watered daily, but if the garlic is planted in the garden, water thoroughly once a week in dry weather.

When the garlic leaves lose their colour in late summer, dig them up carefully, taking care not to damage the bulbs. Shake the soil off and lay them out in a dry sunny place.

When they have ripened store them in a net bag or make a string by plaiting the leaves together and hang them up in a cool, dry place, such as a garage.

Did you know?

Garlic can be used for many different things (apart from keeping off vampires). It is a herb used in medicine, and in the First World War its juice helped to make wounds heal.

Recipe

Garlic and Bacon Pasta

(4 people)

Garlic is a mainstay of French and Italian cooking and has been used for thousands of years – even the Ancient Egyptians found it handy in the kitchen.

> 1 lb tagliatelle pasta
> 4 cloves garlic
> ¼ lb bacon
> 2 tablespoons olive oil
> 1 egg
> Freshly ground pepper
> Grated Parmesan or Cheddar cheese

- Bring a large saucepan of water to the boil and put in the pasta.

Meanwhile
- Peel and slice the garlic cloves into very small pieces.
- Chop the bacon into small pieces.
- Heat the olive oil in the frying pan and fry the garlic until brown.
- Add the bacon and continue cooking until the bacon is tender.

- Drain the pasta in a colander, return to the saucepan and shake over a gentle heat until dry.
- Take it off the heat, add the bacon and garlic and stir well.
- Beat the egg, add the freshly ground pepper and pour over the pasta, stir and serve immediately with grated cheese.

JERUSALEM ARTICHOKES

Ideal conditions   Sunny and dry with good drainage
Time taken   6 months
Sow in   March/early April

You will have to grow these outside as Jerusalem artichokes can reach seven feet high – they are the Triffids of vegetables.

Jerusalem artichokes need well-manured soil – one bucketful of compost or a handful of granular fertiliser per square metre dug in about three weeks before planting. Just before sowing add one handful of fish manure and one handful of sulphate of potash and rake in.

Make holes 15cm deep and 30cm apart, place an artichoke tuber at the bottom of each and re-fill the holes.

As they grow, knock in a 1.5m stake beside each plant and tie the stem to it to stop the artichoke being blown over by the wind.

Most of the artichokes will have grown underground by the end of October so the stems can be cut down and the tubers dug up and stored or, if you have the room, left in the ground for digging up later.

Recipe

Artichoke Provençal

(4 people)
This is a dish from the South of France which goes well with roast meats such as lamb and pork.

> 1 lb artichokes
> 1 teaspoon lemon juice
> 2 tomatoes
> 1 tablespoon olive oil
> 1 clove garlic (peeled and chopped)
> 1 teaspoon chopped basil

- Peel the artichokes and cut them into even-sized pieces.
- Cook in boiling water, to which has been added the lemon juice, until they are almost tender.
- Drain in a colander, return to the saucepan and shake over a gentle heat until dry.
- Skin the tomatoes by immersing them in boiling water and peeling off the skin when it splits.
- Place the artichokes in a pan of hot oil.
- Chop the tomatoes and add them with the chopped garlic and basil to the pan.
- Cook gently until the sauce thickens.

Did you know?

There are two popular artichokes – the Jerusalem artichoke comes from North America and the Globe artichoke comes from the Mediterranean. The heads of the Globe artichoke can be eaten or used in flower arrangements.

LEEKS

Ideal conditions	Well-drained soil in open position
Time taken	8 months
Sow in	March

We like leeks – their mild oniony flavour is delicious, especially with chicken, and they are quite easy to grow.

Leeks need well-manured soil – one bucketful of compost or a handful of granular fertiliser per square metre dug in about three weeks before planting. Just before sowing add two handfuls of fish manure and rake in.

In mid-March, prepare a seed bed by raking until the soil is very fine and all the weeds and stones have been removed. Tread the soil down until it is firm and make a drill 1cm deep.

Mix the seed with an equal amount of sand and sprinkle thinly along the row. Cover with soil.

By the middle of June the leeks should be dug up carefully for re-planting. With a dibber make holes 15cm deep and 15cm apart.

Cut off the top quarter of the leaves and the bottom half of the roots and pop the remains in a hole. Fill the hole with water – there is no need to re-fill it with earth.

At the end of July scatter a handful of granular fertiliser every square metre. At the same time, earth up the leeks by drawing earth round them or tie a collar of thick paper or card round them so that the stems become white.

They should be ready to eat by November, but you can leave them in the ground until you want them.

Did you know?

Leeks can grow up to 9 lb in weight. In some parts of England leek growing competitions are organised to find the largest leeks.

Recipe

Leeks in Cheese Sauce

Despite the attractions of chicken and leek pie, we thought you might like to do this tasty lunch-time snack.

> 1 lb leeks
> 2 oz butter/margarine
> 2 oz wholemeal flour
> 1 pint milk
> 4 oz Cheddar or Lancashire cheese
> 1 teaspoon Dijon mustard
> 1 teaspoon chopped basil
> 1 tomato

- Trim off the root, hard base, top and outer leaves of each leek.
- Chop into 1cm slices and wash **very** thoroughly.
- Place the leeks in a saucepan with sufficient boiling water to cover them and cook until tender. Steam them if possible.
- Drain in a colander, return to the saucepan and shake over a gentle heat until dry.

Meanwhile
- Melt the butter/margarine in a saucepan. Add sufficient flour to leave the sides dry when mixed together.
- Add the milk, a little at a time, stirring continuously.
- When it becomes a thick sauce, without lumps, add the cheese, basil and mustard.
- Cook until smooth, stirring all the time.

- Place the leeks in a greased, oven-proof dish and pour the sauce over them.
- Decorate with slices of tomato and grill for five minutes.

LETTUCE

Ideal conditions	Open position or grow-bag
Time taken	2–3 months
Sow in	Early April onwards

Lettuces are extremely easy to grow but do best in rich, moist soil.

As they like well-manured soil, dig in one bucketful of compost or a handful of granular fertiliser per square metre about three weeks before planting. Just before sowing add two handfuls of fish manure and rake in.

Prepare a seed-bed by raking until the soil is very fine and all the weeds and stones removed. Tread the soil down until it is firm and make a drill 1cm deep.

Mix the seed with an equal amount of sand and sprinkle thinly along the row or directly into a grow-bag. Sow a small quantity at fortnightly intervals so you get a continuous supply of lettuces. Cover the seeds very lightly and water thoroughly.

When the seedlings are large enough to handle, transplant them or thin them out to 20cm apart. Make a hole with a dibber, pop the lettuce in and tread down firmly.

Keep them well-watered in dry weather and feed with a liquid fertiliser (follow the manufacturer's instructions).

When they are firm in the middle, cut them, preferably early in the morning or just before eating.

Green Salad

(4 people)
Although lettuce is a common ingredient of salad, used as decoration (or even cooked), a green summer salad is always welcome.

> 1 lettuce
> 1 green pepper
> 10 spring onions
> ½ cucumber
> Handful of parsley sprigs
> 1 tablespoon chopped chives
> French dressing

- Wash the lettuce thoroughly, a leaf at a time.
- Shake dry and chill in the refrigerator for an hour.
- Wash the remaining vegetables.
- Remove the core and seeds of the green pepper and chop it into thin slices.
- Slice the lettuce into thin strips about 7cm long.
- Slice the cucumber into thin rounds.
- Top and tail the onions.
- Place the lettuce on a plate and arrange the remaining vegetables in a pattern.
- Sprinkle with parsley and chives.
- Serve with French dressing.

Did you know?

The most interesting thing about lettuce (Yawn!) is that there are at least 18 varieties – how many can you grow?

MARROWS

Ideal conditions	Sunny position or grow-bag
Time taken	5 months
Sow in	May

You can grow some huge marrows which can be stuffed and cooked in various ways.

Marrows need very well-manured soil – two bucketfuls of compost or two handfuls of granular fertiliser per square metre dug in about three weeks before planting. Just before sowing add two handfuls of fish manure and rake in.

Fill a 6cm peat pot with potting compost and push two seeds into the soil (1cm deep) on opposite sides of the pot. Make sure the pointed end is uppermost.

Put in a warm place and water sparingly. If both seeds germinate, remove the weakest one. In June, when all danger of frost is passed, they can be planted outside or into a grow-bag.

Water regularly in dry weather and feed every ten days with a liquid fertiliser (follow the manufacturer's instructions).

If you want large marrows, thin them down to four or five a plant.

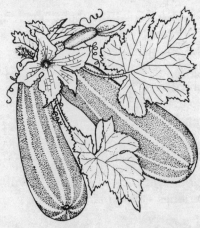

Recipe

Marrow and Ginger Jam

This is a very unusual jam so why not make some for the school fête or Autumn Fayre.

> 2 lb marrow
> ¼ pint water
> 1 oz root ginger
> 2 lemons
> 2 lb sugar

- Peel the marrow and cut the flesh into small cubes.
- Steam or cook in ¼ pint boiling water until just cooked.
- Hammer the ginger to break up the fibres and tie it up in a muslin or cheesecloth bag.
- Grate the lemon rind and then squeeze out the juice.
- Mix the rind gratings, juice, sugar, marrow and ginger bag together.
- Leave overnight in a cool place.
- Remove the bag, place all the ingredients in a saucepan and bring to the boil, stirring continuously.
- Simmer until the marrow pieces have become clear and the syrup has thickened.
- Place in jam jars and cover tightly.

Did you know?

To find out if marrows are not too old, push your thumbnail in the rib of the vegetable just above the stalk. If it penetrates easily – it is just right. If it is hard – don't bother to eat it!

Ideal conditions	Greenhouse or grow-bag in a cold frame
Time taken	6 months
Sow in	March

A little tricky to grow, but well worth it as fresh melons are scrumptious.

Except during July and August, the melons will need to be in a greenhouse or cold frame. You can make a cold frame by placing a 30cm high wooden square round a grow-bag and covering it with glass.

In March, sow melon seeds in peat pots. Keep them moist and place in a warm place such as an airing cupboard. When the seeds germinate, place them on a warm windowsill.

In June, when all danger of frost has passed, plant them into the growbag or greenhouse. They should be planted in a small mound to drain water away from the roots.

When the shoots are a metre long, pinch out the tip. Male and female flowers will then appear on side shoots. When five female flowers have developed (look for the mini-melon behind the flower), take a petal from a male flower and place it on the female flower to transfer the pollen.

Once the melons have set (started to swell) pinch out the tips of the side shoots.

As they swell, pinch the smallest one off so there are only four per plant. They will need watering thoroughly every day and feeding once a week with liquid fertiliser (follow the manufacturer's instructions).

Harvest the melons as they ripen (the stalk nearest the melon will begin to split).

Recipe

Melon Surprise

(4 people)

A delicately flavoured way of serving melon which would be nice for lunch on a hot summer day.

1 melon
1 large orange
1 large lemon
4 oz castor sugar
2 oz sultanas
1 oz candied peel
2 oz whole hazelnuts
½ teaspoon ground ginger
2 tablespoons triple strength orange flower water

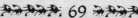

- Squeeze the orange and the lemon to extract the juice.
- Place in saucepan with the castor sugar.
  Dissolve over a low heat.
- Add sultanas, peel, hazelnuts and ginger.
- Boil fiercely for two minutes.
  Remove from the heat and stir in the orange flower water.
- Leave to cool.
- Slice the melon, remove the seeds and cut into chunks (or use a melon scoop to make melon balls).
- Spoon syrup over the melon and serve.

Did you know?

Melons are native to tropical Africa, and a watermelon has grown up to 200 lb in weight.

MINT

Ideal conditions	Semi-shade or pot
Time taken	1–2 months
Sow in	April

There are several different varieties of this common herb which originated in the East and arrived in this country via North Africa. Try growing different sorts – spearmint (tastes like chewing gum), peppermint and apple mint are easily obtainable.

Mint can get out of hand in the garden, so contain the roots by burying a large plant pot or bucket and growing the mint in that. Alternatively, grow it in a 30cm plant pot filled with potting compost.

As mint is difficult to grow from seed, it is probably best to buy a small plant from a garden centre or persuade a gardening friend to let you have a root (most people are only too glad to get rid of some!).

In the garden, dig a large hole, bury the plant pot or bucket and fill it with soil which has been mixed with two handfuls of peat or compost. Make a hole the size of the mint root in the centre of the pot. Plant the mint in the hole, re-fill with earth and firm down well.

When the flower buds appear, pinch them off to encourage more leaves.

Pick the leaves when they are young and hang them up to dry in a well-ventilated room for winter use.

Recipe

Mintade

(per person)
This is like lemonade but has a lovely minty flavour.

6 tablespoons chopped mint leaves
1 teaspoon castor sugar
¼ pint water
1 orange
1 lemon
500ml bottle of soda water
2 ice cubes

- Place the mint and sugar in a saucepan with the water and bring to the boil.
- Cool.
- Squeeze the orange and the lemon to extract the juice and add it to the mint water.
- Strain the liquid through a sieve.
- Add the soda water, ice cubes and serve.

Did you know?

A sprig of mint should be added to new potatoes and peas when they are boiled. When mixed with honey and lemon juice mint makes a delicious sauce for roast lamb.

MUSHROOMS

Ideal conditions	Semi-shade indoors
Time taken	8 weeks
Sow in	Any time

To grow mushrooms you do not need a garden – you do not even have to have 'much room'. Some garden centres sell starter packs – you could add it to your birthday present list!

Mushrooms need a constant temperature of between 70° and 80° Fahrenheit, so grow them in a deep seed tray or large bucket in a shed or garage – or even indoors under the bed!

Place mushroom compost in the container (horse manure which has matured is better, though a bit smelly) and firm it down. Scatter the mushroom spawn on top and water sparingly. Make sure it is wet, but not soaked.

Cover the container with black plastic sheeting.

Leave for a week or two in the correct temperature, watering very sparingly. You should see greyish threads (called mycellium) spreading across the surface. After two more weeks, cover the mycellium with 2–3cm of potting compost. Continue to water very sparingly and make sure there is good ventilation.

When the mushrooms come up, twist the stalk off at the base. Re-fill the stalk holes with compost and water thoroughly to start off a second crop.

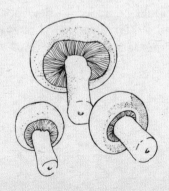

Recipe

Mushrooms with Nutmeg

(per person)
This is an ideal dish for a light lunch or tea.

> 5 large mushrooms
> Grated nutmeg
> Freshly ground pepper
> Butter/margarine
> Slice of wholemeal toast

- Preheat the oven to 190°C.
- Take off the mushroom stalks (use them for flavouring stews and other dishes).
- Wash and dry the mushrooms.
- Lay them in a baking dish with the gills uppermost.
- Sprinkle with a pinch of grated nutmeg and a twist of the peppermill.
- Place a tiny portion of butter or margarine in the centre of each mushroom.
- Cook in the oven for 20 minutes.
- Serve on hot buttered toast.

Did you know?

Mushrooms are an extremely versatile vegetable – they can be used on their own, in stuffings, soups, casseroles or in pies with meat, cheese and eggs.

Ideal conditions	Sunny, light soil
Time taken	7 months
Sow in	March

You can grow onions from seeds, but they are easiest from small bulbs called 'sets'.

Onions need well-manured soil – one bucketful of compost or a handful of granular fertiliser per square metre dug in about three weeks before planting. Just before sowing add two handfuls of fish manure and rake in.

Make a drill 2–3cm deep and push the sets gently into the soil and cover lightly. Check daily for a week or so as birds seem to like pulling them up (or the worms push them out!). Until they have rooted some will need pushing back.

In dry weather, water thoroughly once a week until September when they should start to ripen.

At the beginning of October, fold the leaves over and let them dry off. Dig up the onions and lay them in a sunny spot to dry for a month. Turn them over after a fortnight. They can then be stored in trays (or plaited into strings) in a frost-free place until ready for eating.

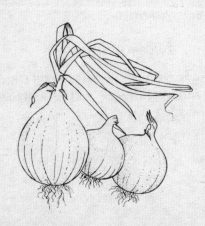

Recipe

Caramel Onions

(4 people)

Onions seem to be used in almost every savoury dish, so it is nice to have one where onions are cooked on their own. Serve this as an accompaniment to roast meats.

> 1 lb onions
> 2 oz butter/margarine
> 2 teaspoons brown sugar
> ½ pint chicken stock

- Choose 12 small onions about the size of ping-pong balls.
- Cut off the roots and stems and peel off the outer brown leaves.
- Melt the butter/margarine in a saucepan and add the onions.
- Cook them, shaking the pan gently for about five minutes until they are brown all over.
- Sprinkle the sugar over the onions and cook in the same way for a further five minutes.
- Add the chicken stock, cover with a lid and simmer until tender (about 25 minutes).

Did you know?

In the 17th Century onions were believed to: 'procure sleep, help digestion, cure acid belching ... and promote insensible perspiration'.

Ideal conditions	Semi-shade or deep pots and tubs
Time taken	3 months
Sow in	April

This is one of the essential herbs and all sorts of stories have grown up around it. It is supposed to be difficult to grow as the seeds can take up to two months to germinate.

Soak the seeds in water overnight before planting.

If growing in a pot, fill it with potting compost, sprinkle a few seeds on top and water. Cover with glass and a newspaper and place it on a window sill. Check every day and keep the soil just moist. When the seeds germinate, remove the glass and thin out to the strongest seedling.

In the garden make a drill 1cm deep. Mix the seed with an equal quantity of sand and sprinkle thinly along the row. Cover and firm gently.

When the seedlings are 5–10cm high thin them out to 20cm apart.

Parsley should be picked fresh when needed, but it can be dried for winter use. Try freezing sprigs in ice-cubes and packing in freezer bags. You can then use one at a time in your cooking.

Parsley Butter

(per person)

A delicious butter which can be added to jacket potatoes or grilled fish.

> ½ oz butter
> 1 tablespoon chopped parsley
> ½ teaspoon lemon juice
> Freshly ground pepper

- Soften the butter by leaving it in a warm place for an hour.
- Chop the parsley and blend with the butter.
- Add the lemon juice and a twist of the pepper mill.
- Continue blending until all the liquid has gone.
- Place on hot baked potatoes or grilled fish.

Did you know?

It is said to be unlucky to move parsley – so make sure you plant it where you want it to grow! If you chew parsley, it will take away the smell of garlic on your breath.

Ideal conditions	Open, sunny site
Time taken	10 months
Sow in	January–March

Parsnips are not as popular as they should be – or as they once were. They were used like potatoes before the 16th Century when the first potatoes arrived from America.

Parsnips are not really suitable for growing in boxes or pots, so find a piece of land at least 2m square which you can use for a year since they take a long time to grow.

Fertilise with granular fertiliser (one handful per square metre) and make drills 2cm deep and 25cm apart. Sow the seed thickly in each row and cover with soil.

When the plants are 4–5cm high, thin them out to 4cm apart by removing the weakest ones.

If the weather is dry in the early months of growth, water thoroughly once a week.

After the first winter frosts, dig up the parsnips as you need them.

Roasted Parsnips

(4 people)
You can eat the green leaves of parsnips as a green vegetable in the same way as you eat cabbage. Here is a recipe for the more common part which is excellent with a roast dinner, especially chicken. You should have help from an adult because this recipe uses very hot fat.

1 lb of parsnips
Sufficient oil to cover the bottom of a roasting pan to 1cm deep

- Place a pan of oil in the oven with the roast if there is insufficient room for the parsnips in the same pan as the roast.
- Scrape the parsnips and cut into quarters lengthways (cut these again if it is a large parsnip).
- Place them in a pan (or round the roast) and baste (pour or brush hot fat over the parsnips).
- Cook in the oven until brown and tender (about 45–60 minutes at 190°C).
- Drain them on a piece of kitchen paper before serving.

Did you know?

Like Brussels sprouts, parsnips are sweeter after the first winter frosts as the cold breaks down the starchy cells, converting them into sugar.

Ideal conditions	Sunny, open position or grow-bag
Time taken	3 months
Sow in	March onwards

Peas are not difficult to grow although you will need to make sure you have the right variety for the time of year you are planting.

Peas need well-manured soil – one bucketful of compost or a handful of granular fertiliser per square metre dug in about three weeks before planting. Just before sowing add two handfuls of fish manure and rake in.

Make a drill 2cm deep, plant the peas 6cm apart and cover them lightly. Birds are partial to pea seedlings so protect your plants by stretching cotton tied to sticks over them.

As they grow, the peas will want support. Push pea sticks into the ground beside them and wind the plants through.

Water thoroughly once a week in dry weather and lay a mulch of 2cm deep lawn clippings (or strips of black polythene) around the plants to conserve moisture.

Pick the pods when the peas inside are large enough to eat, taking care not to leave any, otherwise the plant will stop producing new ones.

Paprika Peas

(4 people)

Fresh peas from the garden boiled with mint are super. Here is a different recipe which is quite interesting when served with grilled meat or fish.

1 clove of garlic
2 onions
1 large tin tomatoes
2 teaspoons paprika
1 lb shelled peas
2 tablespoons tomato purée
Freshly ground pepper
Parsley sprigs

- Skin and crush the garlic.
- Peel the onions and chop into small pieces.
- Place in a saucepan with the tomatoes and paprika.
- Boil and then simmer for 15 minutes, mashing the tomatoes frequently.
- Add the peas, tomato purée and freshly ground pepper.
- Cook for five minutes, place in a serving dish, sprinkle with parsley sprigs and serve.

Did you know?

Peas belong to the **Leguminosae** family – of which there are over 7000 different species, all producing seeds in pods.

Ideal conditions	Warm sheltered position in grow-bag or pot
Time taken	5–6 months
Sow in	March

Peppers are available in three colours – red, green and yellow – so try to grow some of each. They are not too difficult to cultivate, but require plenty of food, water and sun – don't we all!

In March, fill a seed tray with potting compost and firm it down. Sow the seeds about 2cm apart and cover with 1–2cm of earth. Water well and cover with a sheet of glass. Wipe the moisture from the glass daily and remove when the seedlings have germinated. Place in as light a position as possible.

When the peppers have three leaves, plant them into separate 10cm peat pots filled with compost. If they are to be grown outside harden them off from mid-May onwards.

By June the roots should be showing through the peat pot and they are ready for sowing 40cm apart in grow-bags or one per 15cm pot.

They will need support, so place a cane in the pot or put in a grow-bag support.

Water regularly (but make sure they are not waterlogged) and feed weekly with a liquid fertiliser (follow the manufacturer's instructions).

Pinch out the first few flowers to encourage larger flowers and spray the underside of the leaves with water every two days to reduce the water loss and annoy red spiders which seem to like peppers.

Did you know?

Peppers originally came from Central and South America. The hottest ones, called chillies, are dried and ground up to make cayenne pepper.

Recipe

Stuffed Peppers

(4 people)

Here is a tasty dish which is surprisingly substantial and makes a good lunch-time meal.

4 large peppers	1 dessertspoon olive oil
4 oz long grain brown rice	1 teaspoon oregano
1 small onion	Freshly ground pepper
2 oz mushrooms	1 medium egg
4 oz bacon	

- Preheat the oven to 175°C.
- Slice the bottom from the peppers and remove the seeds.
- Place the peppers in a saucepan of sufficient boiling water to cover them and cook for 5 minutes. Drain in a colander and set aside.
- Bring a large pan of water to the boil, add the rice and simmer until tender.

Meanwhile
- Wash the mushrooms, peel the onion, and chop them and the bacon into small pieces.
- In the oil fry one ingredient at a time, starting with the onion and finishing with the mushrooms.
- As each is cooked, place it on a plate on top of the rice saucepan to keep warm.
- When all is cooked (including the rice) place everything except the peppers and egg in the frying pan, add the oregano and freshly ground pepper and cook for five minutes stirring continuously.
- Take off the heat, beat in the egg and stuff the whole mess into the peppers.
- Place in a greased oven-proof dish and bake in the oven for 35 minutes.

POTATOES

Ideal conditions	Light, well-drained soil or barrel
Time taken	3–4 months
Sow in	Late March

Potatoes take up quite a lot of room in the garden, so unless you have a lot of land, only grow a few plants to provide early potatoes, or leave them in the ground for jacket potatoes.

Potatoes can be grown in a barrel which should be about 60cm high and almost as wide. Place 10cm of potting compost in the bottom, place a seed potato on it and cover with 10–15cm of compost. Water well and regularly. As the shoots grow, keep adding more compost so only the tips stick out. Leave a 5cm space at the top of the barrel to make it easier to water. Feed with a liquid fertiliser (follow the manufacturer's instructions).

In the garden, potatoes need well-manured soil – one bucketful of compost or a handful of granular fertiliser per square metre dug in about three weeks before planting. Just before sowing add two handfuls of fish manure and rake in.

If possible, allow the seed potatoes to develop two 5cm long shoots (rub off the extra ones) before planting. You can do this by placing the tubers in a seed tray in a frost free place in January with the eyes upwards.

In late March plant them 10cm deep and 30cm apart with the shoots upwards.

When the shoots are about 20cm high, earth the plants by drawing soil up round the shoot to about 10cm high. Repeat this twice more at three weekly intervals.

In late June/early July, carefully scrape away the soil to see if the new potatoes are larger enough to eat. Take what you want and replace the earth so the others will grow. They should be boiled with mint.

In the Autumn, dig up the potatoes carefully, rub the soil off and store in a frost and draught free place.

Recipe

Duchess Potatoes

(4 people)

As a standard vegetable, there are numerous recipes involving potatoes. Here is one for a special occasion.

> 1 lb potatoes
> 1 oz butter/margarine
> 2 tablespoons milk
> 1 egg
> Freshly ground pepper

- Preheat the oven to 200°C.
- Peel the potatoes and cut into similar sized pieces.
- Place them in a saucepan of boiling water, sufficient to cover them. Cook until they are tender.
- Drain in a colander, return to the saucepan and shake over a gentle heat until dry.
- Push the potatoes through a sieve with the back of a wooden spoon.
- Return to the saucepan, stir in the butter/margarine, milk, beaten egg and season with pepper.
- Beat over a low heat until the potatoes are light and fluffy.
- Put the mixture into a piping bag with a large nozzle.
- Pipe mounds about 8cm high on a greased baking tray.
- Bake in the top of the oven for about 25 minutes until brown.

Did you know?

A potato weighing over 18 lb is said to have been dug up in a Chester garden in 1795.

Ideal conditions	Rich soil or grow-bag in full sun
Time taken	5 months
Sow in	April

Pumpkins are a little difficult to grow in this country as our summers are not always warm enough. However, they are such a spectacular plant that it is worth trying one or two in a warm sunny place – a grow-bag or special plot against a south wall would be ideal.

Pumpkins need very well-manured soil – two bucketfuls of compost or two handfuls of granular fertiliser per square metre dug in about three weeks before planting. Just before sowing add two handfuls of fish manure and rake in.

Fill a 6cm peat pot with potting compost and push two seeds into the soil 1cm deep on either side of the pot. Make sure the pointed end is uppermost.

Put in a warm place and water sparingly.

In mid-May begin to harden them off and plant out in June, when all danger of frosts has passed.

Water thoroughly, daily in a grow-bag or twice weekly in the garden. Feed weekly with a liquid fertiliser (follow the manufacturer's instructions).

If you want really large pumpkins, thin them out to one or two per plant.

Did you know?

Large pumpkins can grow up to 30kg. There is a variety called 'Hundredweight' – why not challenge your friends to a competition to see who can grow the biggest?

Recipe

Crunchy Pumpkin Pie

(4 people)
This is a traditional American recipe with a difference.

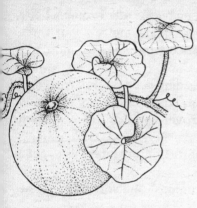

1 small pumpkin
½ teaspoon mixed spice
3 eggs (beaten)
¼ pint milk
4 oz castor sugar
25cm pastry case

Topping
4 oz chopped walnuts
2 oz dark brown soft sugar
2 oz butter/margarine
¼ pint whipped cream

- Preheat the oven to 150°C.
- Peel and slice the pumpkin. Remove the seeds and chop into similar sized pieces.
- Place the pumpkin in a saucepan with ¼ pint of water, cover and boil until tender.
- Make a purée by pushing the pumpkin pieces through a sieve with the back of a wooden spoon.
- Stir in the mixed spice, beaten eggs and sufficient milk to give a thick batter.
- Sweeten to taste and pour into a pie case.
- Bake for 45 minutes in the oven.

Topping
- Melt the butter/margarine in a saucepan and stir in the sugar and walnuts.
- Spoon over the pie and place under a hot grill for a few minutes until it bubbles.
- Serve with whipped cream.

RADISH

Ideal conditions	Sunny position or container
Time taken	4–8 weeks
Sow in	Late March–August

As they are very quick growing (only four weeks in the summer), radishes do not need deep soil, but it has to be rich so they will grow quickly.

Into the top 10cm of soil dig one bucketful of compost or a handful of granular fertiliser per square metre about three weeks before planting. Just before sowing add two handfuls of fish manure and rake in.

Firm the soil by raking and treading it. Make a narrow drill 1cm deep. Mix the seeds with an equal amount of sand and sprinkle thinly along the row. Cover and firm the soil down with the back of the rake.

Sow about a half metre row at fortnightly intervals to get a regular supply of radishes.

In a container place potting compost and sow in the same way as for the garden.

Water twice a week in dry weather (daily in a container) and feed weekly with a liquid fertiliser (follow the manufacturer's instructions).

Recipe

Radish Flowers

We did discover (and try) a recipe for boiled radishes, but it was so awful we thought we would tell you about radish art instead! This is a decorative way of adding them to salads since food is best if it looks good as well as tastes good.

- Remove the stalk and root.
- Make lengthways cuts from the root almost to the stalk or
- Make semi-circular overlapping cuts like fish scales.
- Place in iced water in the refrigerator. The radishes should open up like flowers.

Did you know?

According to Nicholas Culpepper, who died in 1654 and wrote a famous book on herbs, radishes 'sweeten the blood and juices and are good against scurvy'. Scurvy was a disease caused by lack of fresh vegetables and was once common amongst sailors on long voyages as they were unable to carry fresh fruit and vegetables.

Ideal conditions	Sunny position or grow-bags
Time taken	3–4 months
Sow in	End of May/early June

These delicious beans do not like frost or cold conditions so you will have to wait until all danger of frost has passed and the soil warms up.

Runner beans are deep rooting and greedy plants which need well-manured soil. At least three weeks before planting, dig in, 25–30cm deep, one bucketful of compost or a handful of granular fertiliser per square metre. Just before sowing add two handfuls of fish manure plus half a handful of potash and rake in.

To get an early start, plant half the beans in plant pots in April and keep them on a windowsill for planting out later.

Outside, make holes 5cm deep and 20cm apart (ten per grow-bag), pop a bean in each and re-fill the hole. Insert a 2m cane into the ground beside each bean. For a grow-bag you will need a frame or strings for them to grow up.

As beans require plenty of water, give them a good soaking once a week in dry weather, more if they are in a grow-bag. A mulch would be useful in the garden.

Runner beans may want a little assistance to help the flowers to set. Each evening in dry weather spray the plants with water.

The pods must be picked before the beans inside begin to swell. Try and pick all the pods. If you leave any to swell up, the plant will stop producing new ones.

Recipe

Sour Beans

(4 people)

We usually eat bowls of beans, cooked until just tender with a little butter and freshly ground pepper. This is a way of making a little more of them.

> 1 lb runner beans
> 1 small carton yoghurt
> ½ teaspoon grated nutmeg
> 1 teaspoon lemon juice
> Freshly ground pepper

- Wash and trim the ends from the beans, removing any strings from the sides.
- Slice them at an angle into 2cm sections.
- Place them in a saucepan with sufficent boiling water to just cover the bottom. If possible, steam them.
- Drain in a colander, return to the saucepan and shake over a gentle heat until dry.
- Mix in the other ingredients and heat through gently without boiling.

Did you know?

Runner beans come from North America and until about 100 years ago were grown solely for decoration – they can still be used to make good screens in the garden.

SEAKALE BEET

Ideal conditions	Water-retaining soil in the sun
Time taken	3 months
Sow in	April

Another very unusual vegetable which is quite easy to grow. The leaves and stems are the part to eat – either separately or together.

Seakale beet need well-manured soil – one bucketful of compost or a handful of granular fertiliser per square metre dug in about three weeks before planting. Just before sowing add two handfuls of fish manure and rake in.

Make a drill 1cm deep and plant 3 or 4 seeds together in groups 45cm apart. When the seedlings are large enough to handle thin out each group to leave the largest one.

Water thoroughly in dry weather.

Use the young, tender leaves in the centre. Pull them out rather than cutting them as they tend to bleed.

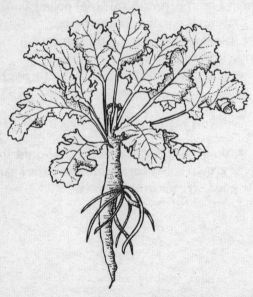

Recipe

Boiled Seakale

(4 people)

This is a simple recipe for making rather a tasty green leaf vegetable dish.

> 1 lb seakale leaves
> 1 oz butter/margarine
> 1 tablespoon single cream
> ¼ teaspoon grated nutmeg
> Freshly ground pepper

- Strip the seakale leaves from the stalks and wash them well. Do not shake dry.
- Place them in a saucepan **without** any water and cook gently for about 15 minutes until tender, stirring occasionally.
- Put in a colander and drain well, pressing out the water.
- Place back in the saucepan, add the cream, butter/margarine and nutmeg. Re-heat over a *very low* heat.
- Season with freshly ground pepper and serve.

Did you know?

Seakale grows wild on some beaches in Hampshire.

SHALLOTS

Ideal conditions	Sunny soil or grow-bag
Time taken	6 months
Sow in	February

These are grown and used in much the same way as onions but have a milder flavour and make good pickles. They can be grown from seed, but are easier grown from small bulbs called 'sets'.

Shallots need manured soil – half a bucketful of compost or a handful of granular fertiliser per square metre dug in about three weeks before planting. Just before sowing add two handfuls of fish manure and rake in.

Make sure the ground is flat and firm. Make a line by placing a stick at each end of the row and tying a length of string between. Push the shallots into the ground at 15cm intervals or make a drill 1cm deep and place them in, covering them up.

As you do for onions, check each day that the bulbs have not come out. If they have, push them back into soil again until they root.

Water thoroughly once a week in dry weather until September. In mid-June give them a feed of liquid fertiliser (follow the manufacturer's instructions).

In September, bend the leaves over. When they turn yellow, dig up the shallot clusters and place them in the sun to ripen. Turn them over each day for a month. Store them in a frost free place until wanted for use.

Recipe

Shallot Vinegar

Although shallots are the right size for making pickled onions or for use in salads instead of onions, this recipe makes a flavoured vinegar for salad dressings.

> 2 oz shallots
> ½ pint white wine vinegar
> 6 peppercorns

- Chop the shallots into small pieces.
- Put all the ingredients in a jam jar and cover it tightly.
- Shake or stir it with a wooden spoon daily for ten days.
- Strain through a sieve and pour into a bottle with a tight fitting cork or cap.

Did you know?

Peppercorns come from an Indian vine. Black peppercorns are the whole of the fruit; when the husks are removed you get white peppercorns.

Ideal conditions	Sunny position
Time taken	3 months
Sow in	Early March

Spinach is quite simple to grow – which is just as well since you need great heaps of leaves to make a meal!

Spinach needs well-manured soil – one bucketful of compost or a handful of granular fertiliser per square metre dug in about three weeks before planting. Just before sowing add two handfuls of fish manure and rake in.

Make a drill 3cm deep, mix the seed with an equal amount of sand and sprinkle it thinly along the row. Cover with soil. After 3–4 weeks thin the seedlings to 8cm apart and three weeks later, thin them to 15cm apart (you can eat the spinach you thin out).

Water thoroughly in dry weather (use a mulch) and feed fortnightly with liquid fertiliser (follow the manufacturer's instructions).

Pick the leaves when they are young, always leaving a few so more will grow.

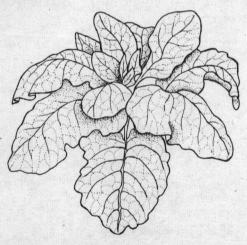

Recipe

Spinach Pancakes

(4 people)

By mixing puréed spinach with pancake batter, you make green pancakes into which you can put a variety of fillings such as cooked bacon and mushroom, cheese and tomato or herbs.

> 1 lb of spinach leaves
> 2 eggs
> 6 oz wholemeal flour
> 1 pint milk
> Freshly ground pepper
> Knob of butter/margarine

- Strip the stalks from the spinach leaves and wash them thoroughly. Do not shake them dry.
- Put them in a saucepan **without** any water and cook gently for ten minutes until tender, stirring occasionally.
- Purée the spinach by pushing it through a sieve with the back of a wooden spoon.
- Whisk together the eggs, flour, milk, pepper and puréed spinach to a smooth batter.
- Melt the knob of butter/margarine in a frying pan, making sure the bottom and sides of the pan are coated.
- Pour in a thin layer of batter mix.
- Cook for a few minutes and turn the pancake over by tossing it in the air (you can turn it over with a wooden spatula – or use the spatula to scrape it off the ceiling!)
- Place the filling on half the pancake and fold it over. Cook for a minute or two on each side and serve.

Did you know?

Spinach originally came from Asia and contains lots of iron – that is what makes Popeye so strong!

STRAWBERRIES

Ideal conditions	Sunny position, grow-bag or container
Time taken	10 months
Sow in	August/September

Everyone likes strawberries and they taste even better if eaten straight from the plant. Some garden centres sell special strawberry barrels or containers which are filled with compost and has the plants popped into holes. You could try growing strawberries in hanging baskets to save room in the vegetable patch.

Strawberries need well-manured soil – one bucketful of compost or a handful of granular fertiliser per square metre dug in about three weeks before planting. Just before sowing add two handfuls of fish manure and rake in.

Dig holes 15cm deep, 15cm wide and 60cm apart. Place a strawberry plant in each, refill and tread down the earth on either side so it is firmly rooted.

When the plants have flowered in Spring, place a mulch of straw or black polythene round them to conserve moisture and keep the fruit clean.

At the same time, sprinkle a handful of fish manure per square metre round the plants and after fruiting sprinkle a similar amount of hoof and horn meal to help strengthen the plants for next year.

You will need to protect the berries from marauding birds by spreading a net over the plants as soon as the fruit forms.

Recipe

Strawberry Ice-cream

Home-made ice-cream is really yummy! It is expensive to make and very fattening so you only make it on special occasions and serve it in small portions.

> ½ lb strawberries
> 3 eggs
> 3 tablespoons icing sugar
> ½ pint thick cream

- Wash and hull the strawberries. (Hulling the strawberry means removing the green stalk.)
- Mash the strawberries to a pulp.
- Separate the egg yolks from the whites.
- Whisk the egg yolks and the sugar together to make thick foam.
- Whip the cream until it is stiff.
- Fold the cream and the mashed strawberries into the egg yolks.
- Whisk the egg whites until they are stiff and fold them in.
- Pour into a mould and freeze for about 5 hours in the freezer or refrigerator ice box.

Did you know?

The name strawberry probably comes from the custom of placing straw between the rows to protect the fruit.

Ideal conditions	Open position
Time taken	5–6 months
Sow in	May–June

This is a very delicious vegetable which can be eaten on its own or added to stews and casseroles.

Dig the soil lightly – there is no need to fertilise if you did so last year. Rake the soil flat. Add half a handful of fish manure per square metre.

Make a drill 1cm deep. Mix the seed with the same amount of sand, sprinkle thinly along the row, cover and water thoroughly.

When the seedlings are 5–10cm high, thin them to 30cm apart.

In dry weather water thoroughly once a week and add a mulch.

They are ready for cooking from October onwards and can be dug up as needed or left in the ground until November when they should be dug up and stored in a frost-free place.

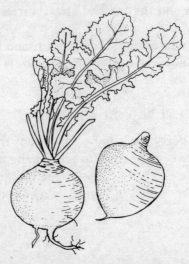

Recipe

Mashed Swede

(4 people)

Here is a simple recipe for swedes as a side dish to a roast dinner.

> 1 small swede
> 2 large carrots
> ½ oz butter/margarine
> ¼ teaspoon grated nutmeg
> Pinch of powdered ginger
> Freshly ground pepper

- Cut off the root and stalk ends and peel the swede.
- Dice into 2cm cubes.
- Scrape the carrots and dice them.
- Place the swede in a saucepan with sufficient boiling water to cover it.
- After 20 minutes cooking, add the carrots. Cook until all the vegetables are tender.
- Drain in a colander, return to the saucepan and shake over a gentle heat until dry.
- Mash with a fork or potato masher until smooth and free of lumps.
- Mix in the rest of the ingredients and serve.

Did you know?

Nutmegs are the seeds of the nutmeg tree which is native to Indonesia. The outer husks of the seeds make another spice called 'mace'.

Ideal conditions	Full sun
Time taken	6 months
Sow in	March

Corn on the cob is very messy to eat. You can barbecue the cobs by wrapping them in tin foil with a knob of butter and placing them on the grill.

Sweetcorn is quite easy to grow, but it does help to have a sunny summer.

Sweetcorn need well-manured soil – one bucketful of compost or a handful of granular fertiliser per square metre dug in about three weeks before planting. Just before sowing add two handfuls of fish manure and rake in.

In March, fill 5cm plant pots with potting compost. Push two seeds into the soil on either side of each pot. Water and place in a warm, light place such as a windowsill. If both seeds germinate, remove the weaker one.

Harden off in mid-May for planting out in June when all danger of frost has passed.

In dry weather give the sweetcorn a thorough soak once a week and a feed of liquid manure (follow the manufacturer's instructions) at the end of July.

About four weeks after flowering the cobs should be ready for eating. The tassel at the end of the cob should turn brown.

Recipe

Corn on the Cob

(per person)
Very simple to do.

> 1 cob of sweetcorn
> Knob of butter
> Freshly ground pepper

- Remove the outer leaves and the silk strands.
- Place in boiling water (do not add salt as this hardens the corn).
- Cook for 15 minutes.
- Spread the cob with melted butter and freshly ground pepper.
- Gnaw.

Did you know?

Sweetcorn has been a food crop in Central America for nearly 4000 years.

TOMATOES

Ideal conditions	Grow-bags or large pots and tubs
Time taken	4 months
Sow in	March

You can grow tomatoes in the garden but they seem to do better in containers against a sunny wall or in the greenhouse. Try the bush varieties in hanging baskets. There are several different types of tomatoes (some are yellow instead of the more familiar red). One we enjoy is the mini-tomato whose fruit grows in clusters to the size of marbles (they are so tasty we eat them straight from the plant).

In March, fill a seed tray with potting compost and firm it down. Sow the seed about 5cm apart and cover with 3mm compost. Water well and cover with a sheet of glass. Wipe the condensation off the glass daily. When the seedlings germinate (7–10 days) remove the glass and place the seed tray in as light a place as possible.

At 3cm high, gently lift the plants out of the compost and plant into separate 10cm peat pots filled with compost. Make sure the top leaves are only a few millimetres above the surface.

In mid-May start to harden them off and plant out in June when all danger of frosts has passed.

The plants will need supporting with a stake or special grow-bag support. As they grow, pinch out the side shoots which form in the leaf joints, unless they are bush tomatoes.

Water daily (but don't let them get waterlogged). A spray with water in the morning or evening will help the flowers to set. When the first tiny green tomatoes appear, feed with a liquid fertiliser (follow the manufacturer's instructions).

Pick the tomatoes as they ripen.

Recipe

Tomatoes on Toast

(per person)

Tomatoes are an essential ingredient in so many dishes that we decided to pick a recipe where they are served on their own. This makes a good lunchtime snack.

> 1 large tomato (or lots of little ones)
> 1 slice wholemeal bread
> Pinch of chopped basil
> Freshly ground pepper

- Slice the tomato into ½cm slices.
- Toast the bread under the grill on one side only.
- Cover the untoasted side with tomato slices.
- Sprinkle with basil and a twist of the peppermill.
- Grill until the tomato is soft.

Did you know?

Tomatoes are fruits, rather than vegetables, and originally came from South America.

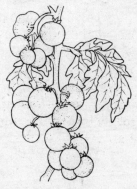

Ideal conditions	Open sunny position
Time taken	2–3 months
Sow in	April

This is a useful vegetable as you can eat the leaves and the roots. They have to be grown quite quickly and eaten when small otherwise they get a bit tough.

Turnips do not need a well-manured soil, but just before sowing add two handfuls of granular fertiliser to the soil and rake it in lightly.

Prepare a fine, firm seed-bed by raking the soil over several times and, if necessary, treading it down before sowing.

Make a drill 1cm deep, mix the seed with an equal quantity of sand, sprinkle thinly along the row, cover and water thoroughly.

When the seedlings are about 10cm high, thin them to 8cm apart and a fortnight later to 15cm apart. You can eat the leaves of the small turnips you pull up.

In dry weather, water thoroughly twice a week.

Turnips should be harvested when they are the size of a golf ball.

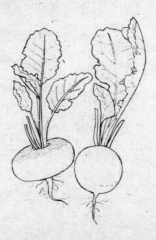

Recipe

Sauted Turnips

(4 people)

Like swedes, turnips are an essential ingredient in good stews and casseroles, but they are equally tasty on their own.

> 1 lb turnips
> 1 tablespoon olive oil
> 2 oz breadcrumbs
> 1 tablespoon chopped parsley
> Freshly ground pepper

- Wash and peel the turnips. Cut them into quarters.
- Place them in a saucepan with sufficient boiling water to cover them and cook for ten minutes.
- Drain in a colander, return to the saucepan and shake over a gentle heat until dry.
- Heat the oil in a frying pan (you will need adult help with this).
- Sauté the turnips gently for ten minutes.
- Stir in the breadcrumbs and chopped parsley.
- Continue cooking until all the oil is absorbed and the breadcrumbs are crisp.
- Season with pepper and serve.

Did you know?

Turnips are not native to the United Kingdom – they originally came from Asia.

VEGETABLE SPAGHETTI

Ideal conditions	Sunny position or grow-bag
Time taken	5 months
Sow in	April

This is rather a strange marrow which, when you cook it, looks like a large heap of spaghetti.

Vegetable spaghetti needs well-manured soil – two bucketfuls of compost or two handfuls of granular fertiliser per square metre dug in about three weeks before planting. Just before sowing add two handfuls of fish manure and rake in.

Fill a 6cm peat pot with potting compost and push two seeds into the soil, 1cm deep, with the pointed end uppermost.

Put in a warm place and water sparingly.

In mid-May, harden off, and in early June plant outside in the garden or in a grow-bag.

Water twice a week (daily in a grow-bag) in dry weather and feed every ten days with a liquid fertiliser (follow the manufacturer's instructions).

The vegetable spaghetti will keep quite well for some months if stored in a cool, frost free place.

Recipe

Boiled Vegetable Spaghetti

(4 people)

This may sound rather uninteresting, but it has a fine delicate flavour.

> 1 vegetable spaghetti
> 1 oz butter/margarine
> Freshly ground pepper

- Cook the spaghetti in boiling water for 20 minutes.
- Cut it in half and scoop out the flesh – it will look like real spaghetti.
- Toss in butter and freshly ground pepper.

Did you know?

Real spaghetti consists of thin, solid pasta strings and is the best known and most popular type of pasta – it is so old that there is a Roman recipe book for pasta dating from AD300.

Ideal conditions	Shady position in garden or large container
Time taken	2–3 months
Sow in	April

Although watercress is usually associated with rivers and ponds, it can be grown in the ground or in a large, shallow container or trough which can be kept well-watered. It does best in the shade.

Dig a trench and fill it (or the container) with peat.

In April, fill a seed tray with seed compost, scatter seed on the surface and cover very lightly. Water, taking care not to disturb the surface. Place on a windowsill and keep moist.

When the seedlings are large enough to handle, re-pot them into 3cm peat pots. From mid-May harden them off for planting outside in June.

Make holes 6cm apart and plant the watercress.

Water two or three times a week, daily in a grow-bag, and feed weekly with liquid fertiliser (follow the manufacturer's instructions).

If the watercress shows signs of flowering, cut off the flowers immediately. Harvest as required by cutting off the tops (more will come).

Recipe

Watercress Butter

(per sandwich)

Watercress can be used to make soup or added to salads – here is an unusual way of pepping up packed lunches. The butter can also be used for spreading on top of crackers and crispbreads for parties, or added to jacket potatoes.

> 1 dessertspoon butter/margarine
> 1 teaspoon chopped watercress
> 1 onion
> Freshly ground pepper

- Soften the butter/margarine by leaving it in a warm place.
- Wash the watercress and chop *very* finely.
- Peel the onion, mince it and squeeze to extract the juice.
- Mix the watercress and butter together. Add onion juice and pepper to taste and blend together.

Did you know?

Watercress is said to be a medicinal herb – in the 17th Century the bruised leaves or juice were placed on the face at night to get rid of spots and pimples!

INDEX OF RECIPES